MEN IN WHITE COATS

MEN IN WHITE COATS

Claude Serre

A WALLABY BOOK
Published by Pocket Books
New York

A Wallaby Book published by
POCKET BOOKS, a division of Simon & Schuster, Inc.
1230 Avenue of the Americas, New York, N.Y. 10020

Published by arrangement with Éditions Jacques Glénat

ISBN: 0-671-54561-2

First Wallaby Books printing March, 1985

10 9 8 7 6 5 4 3 2 1

WALLABY and colophon are registered trademarks
of Simon & Schuster, Inc.

Printed in the U.S.A.

OPERATING ROOM

Surgery

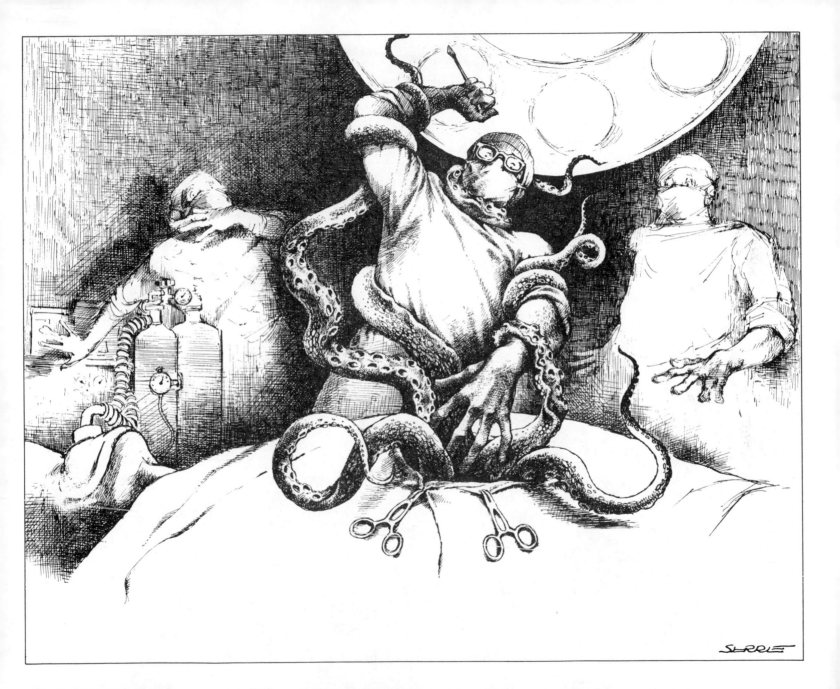

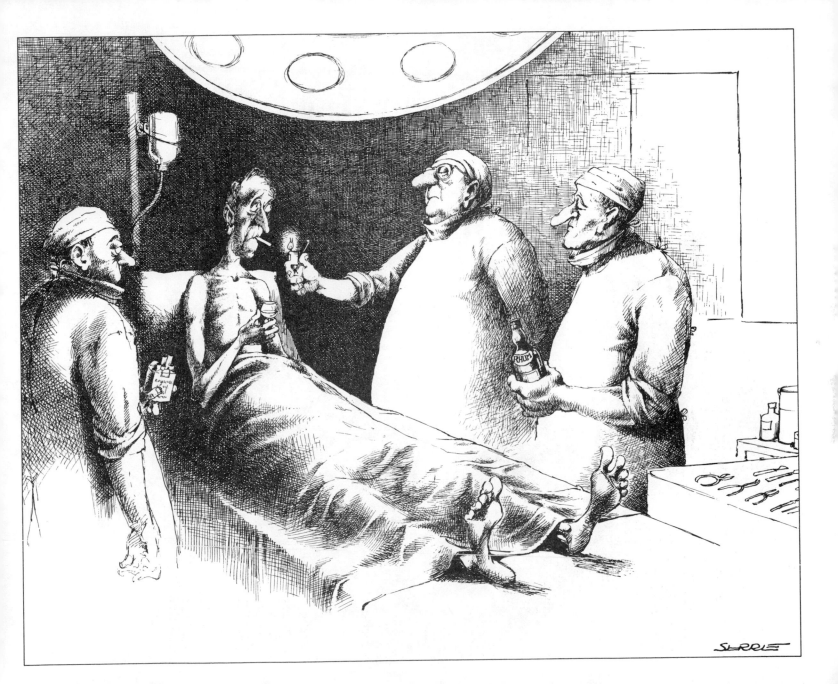

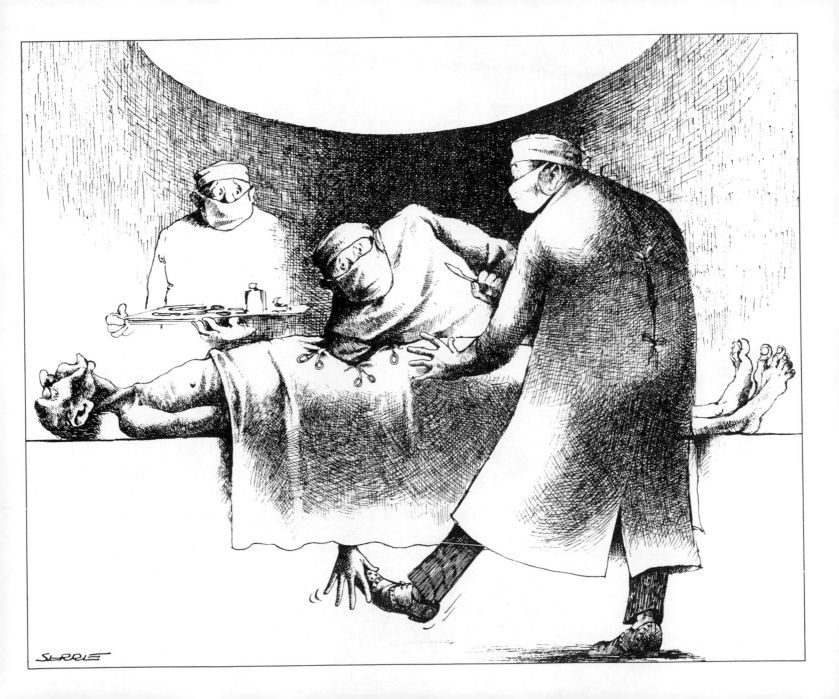

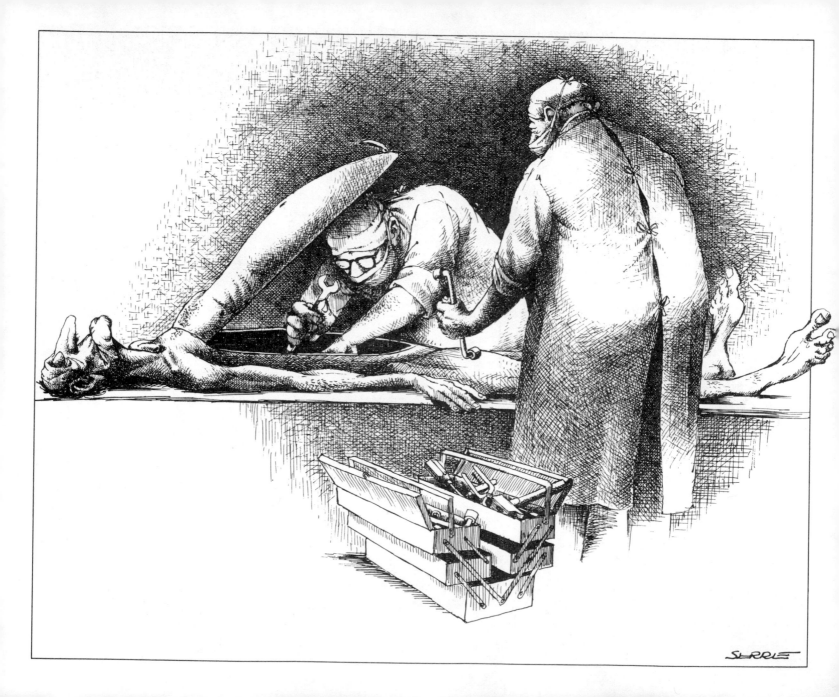

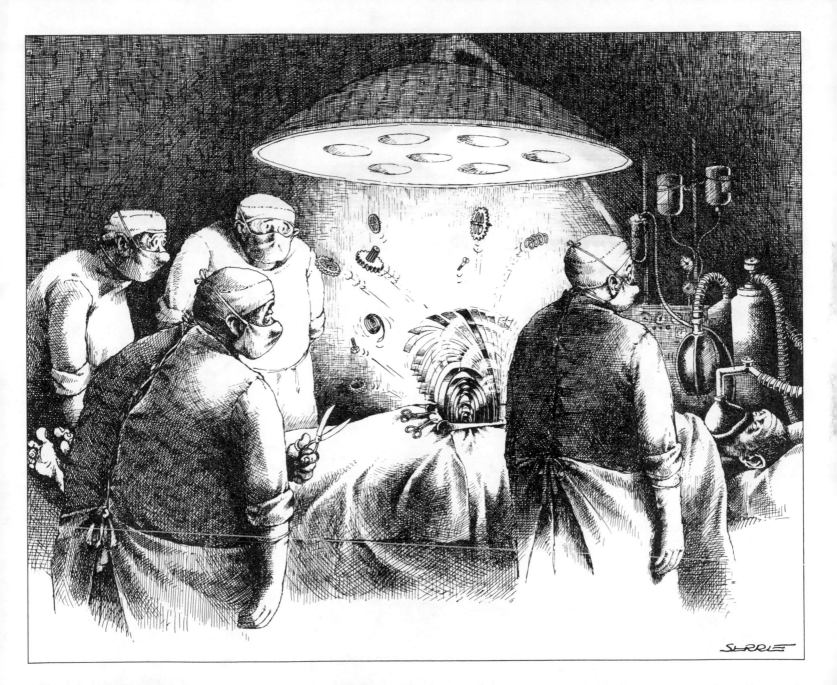

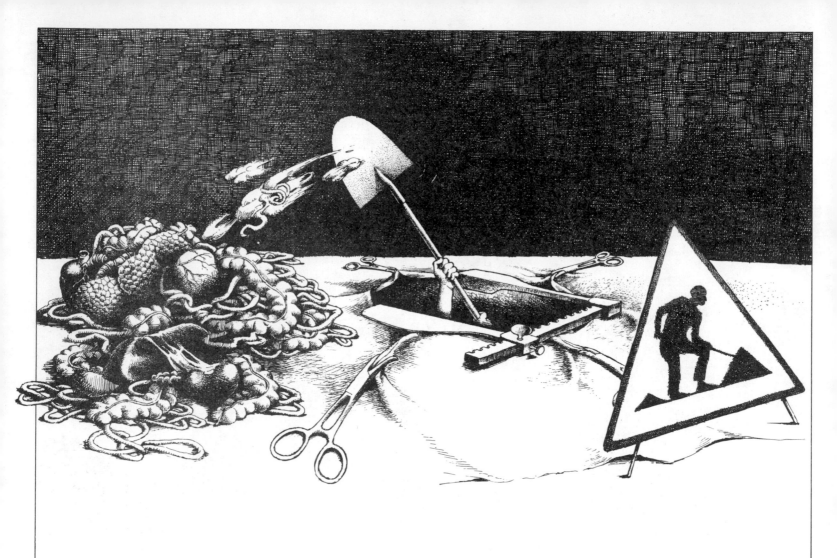

Pharmacy

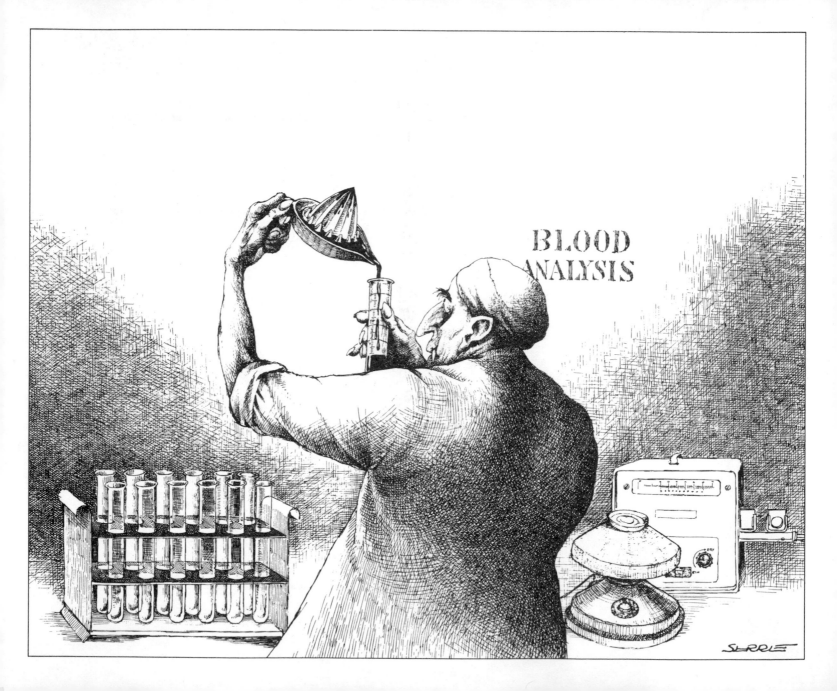

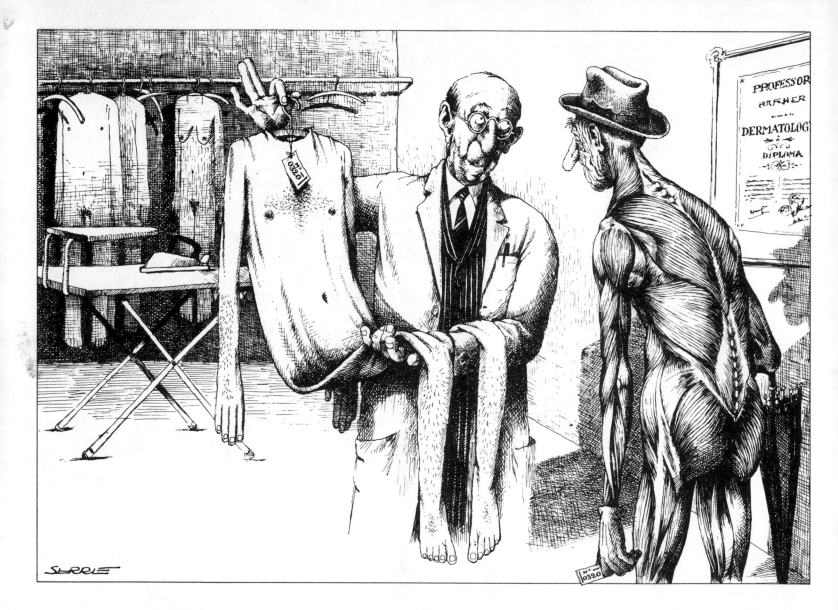

Psychiatry

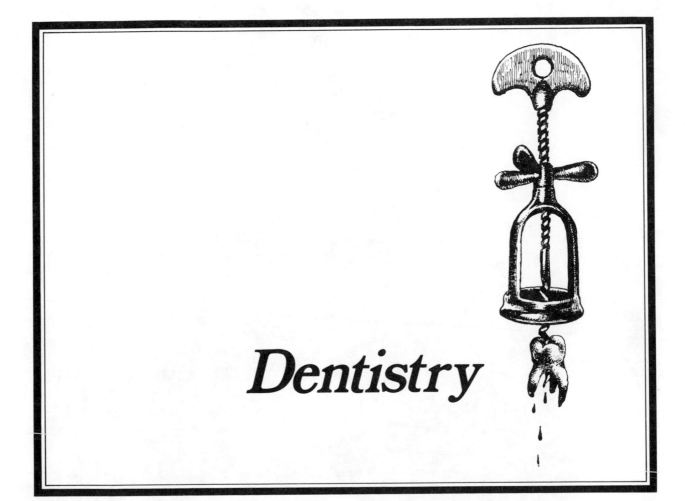

Dentistry

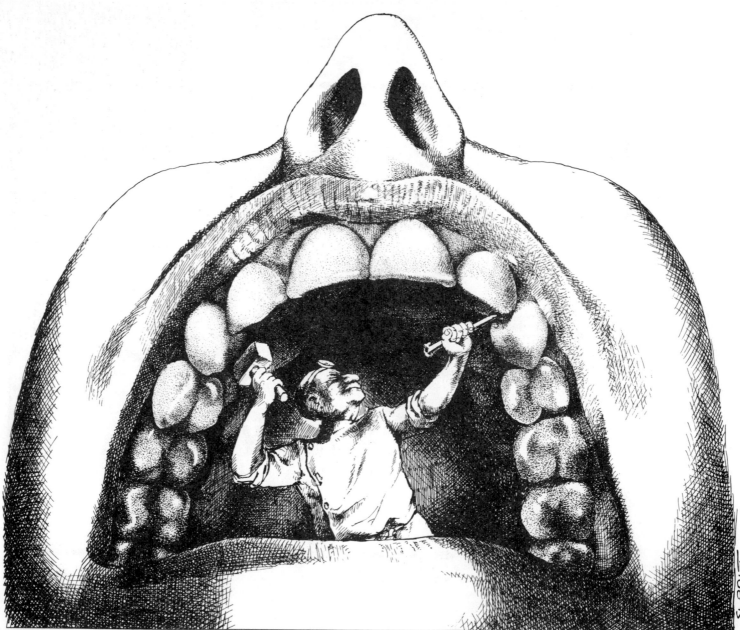

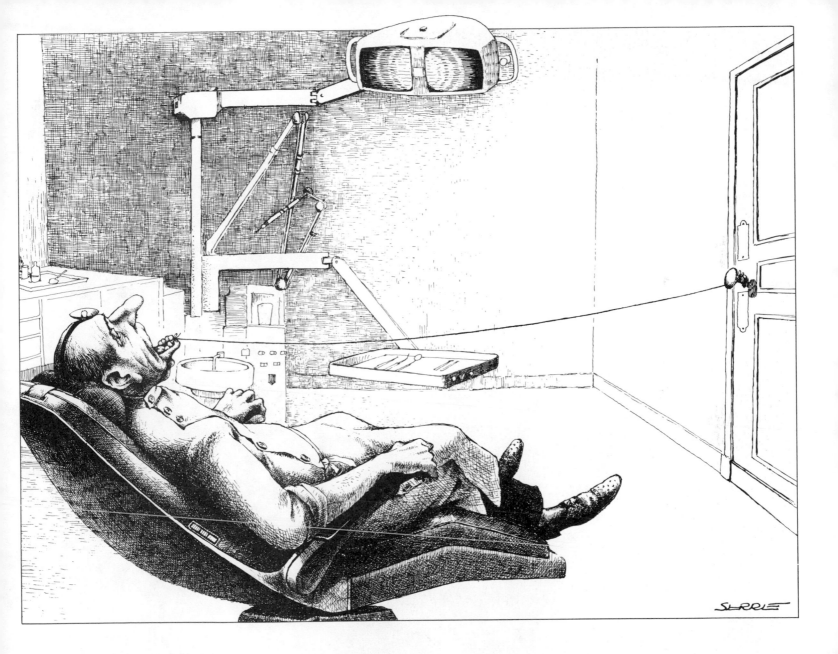

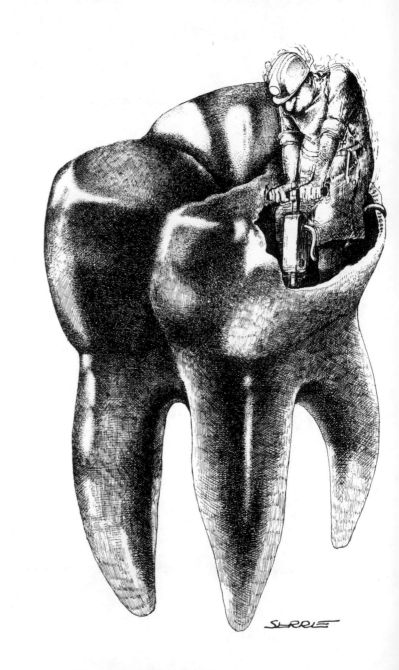

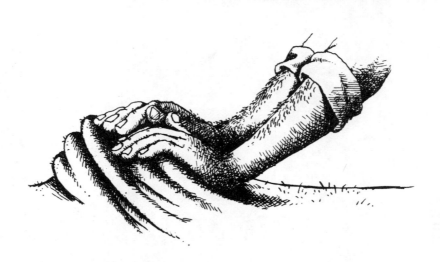

Massage

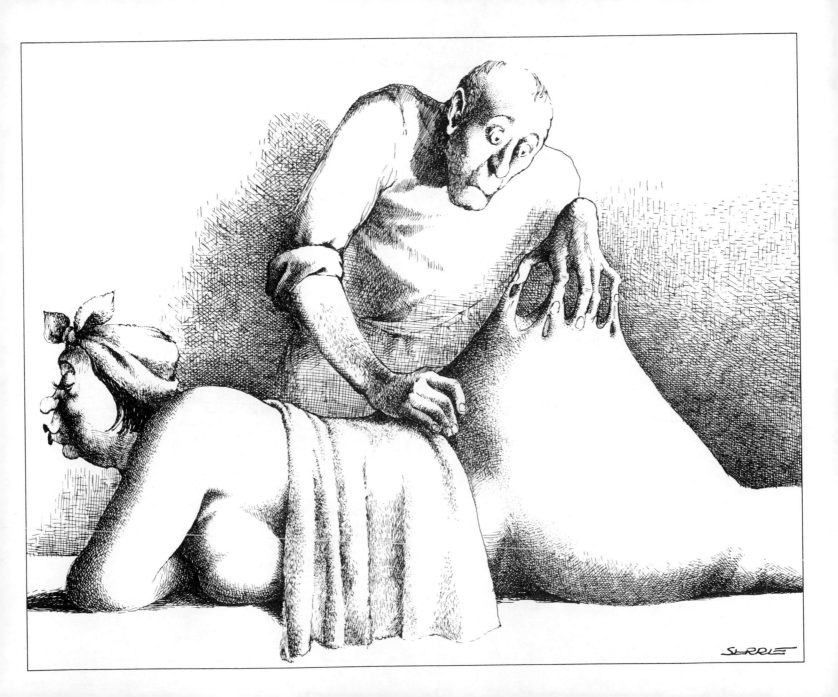

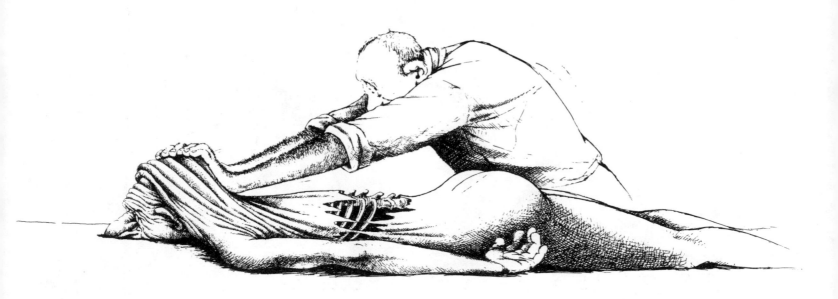

SERRE

General Practice

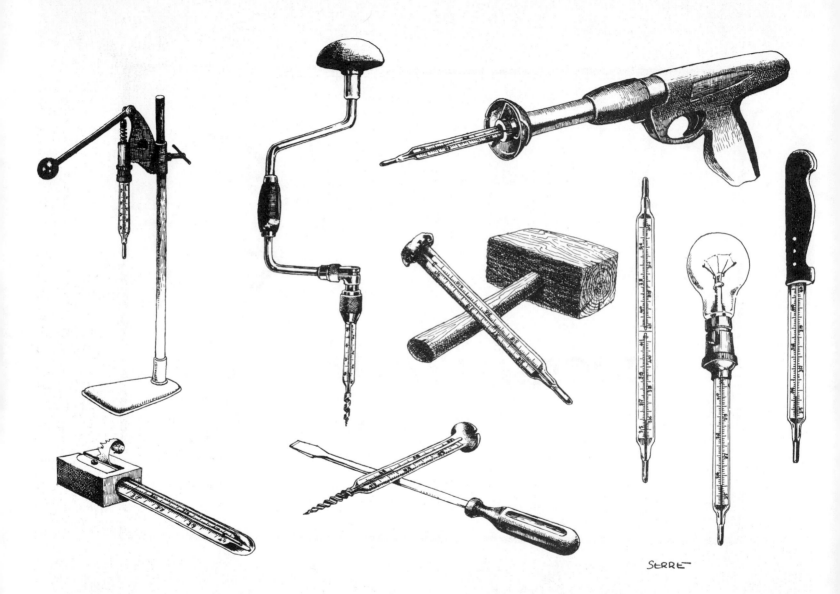

SERRE

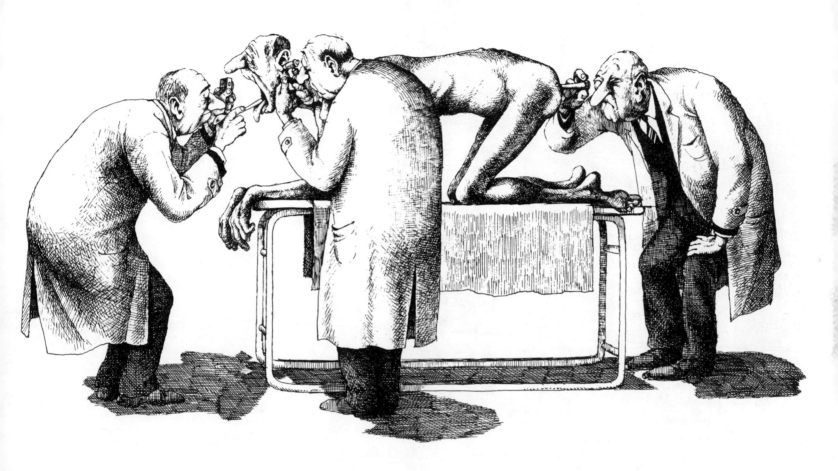

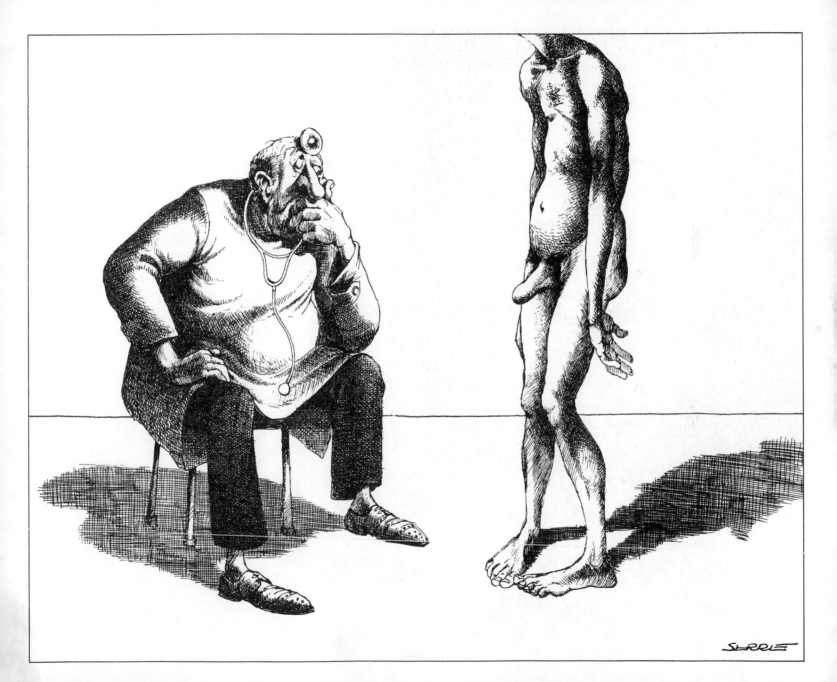

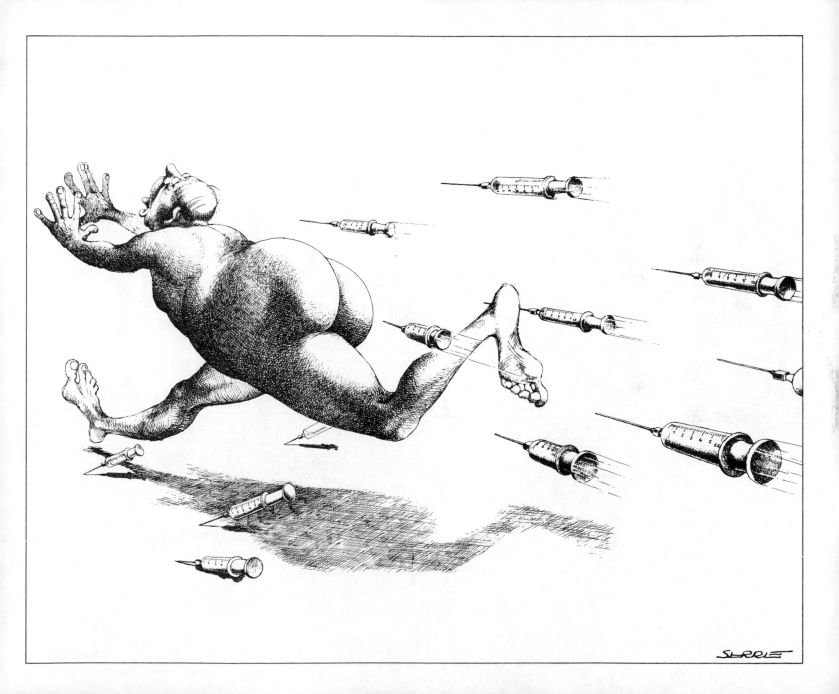

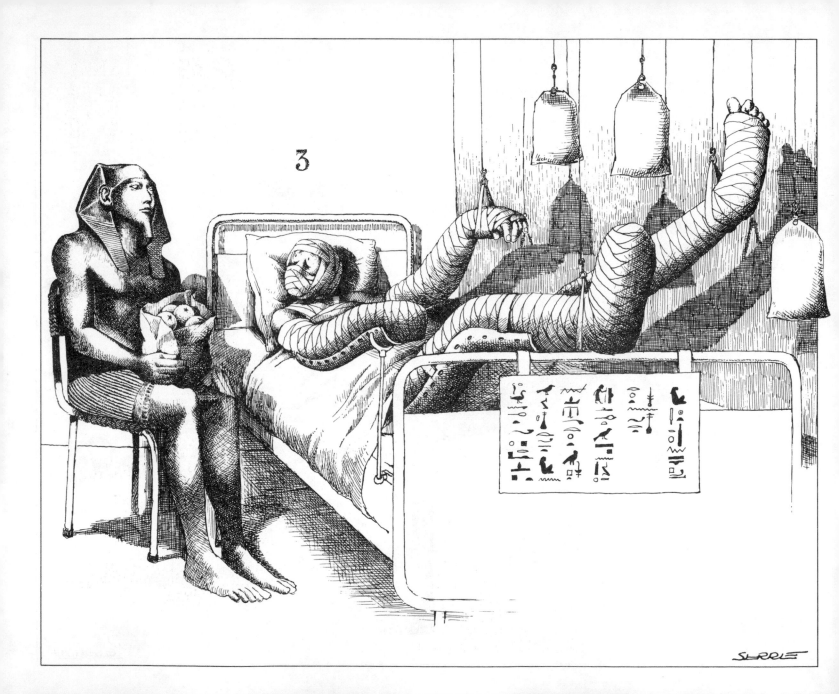

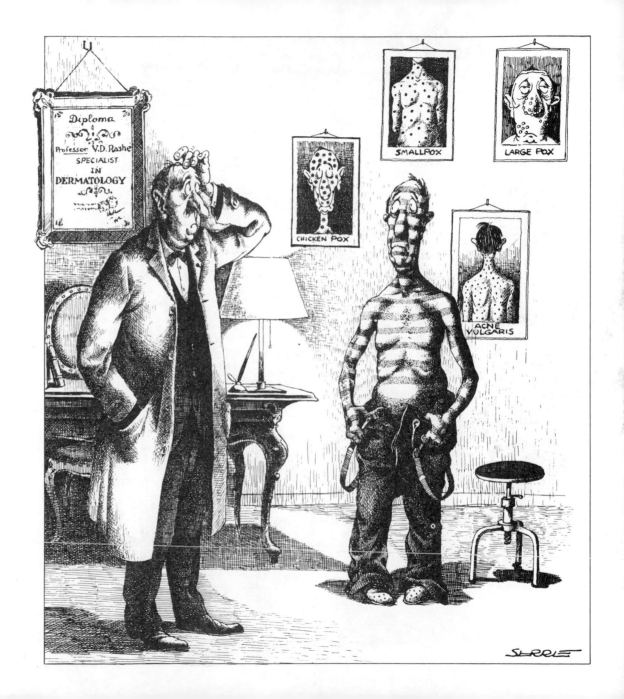

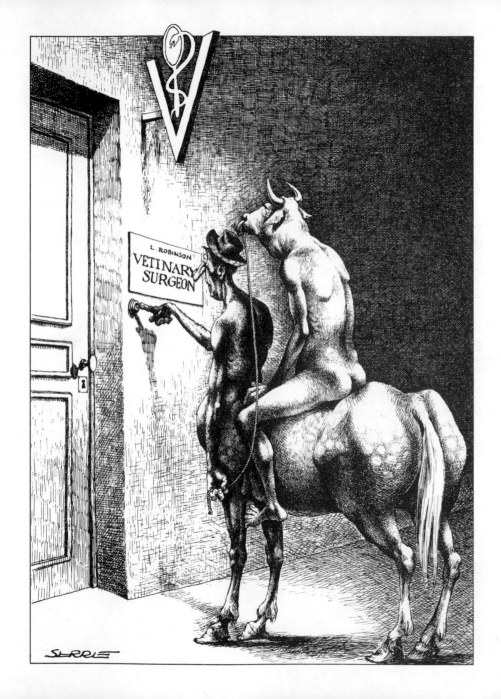

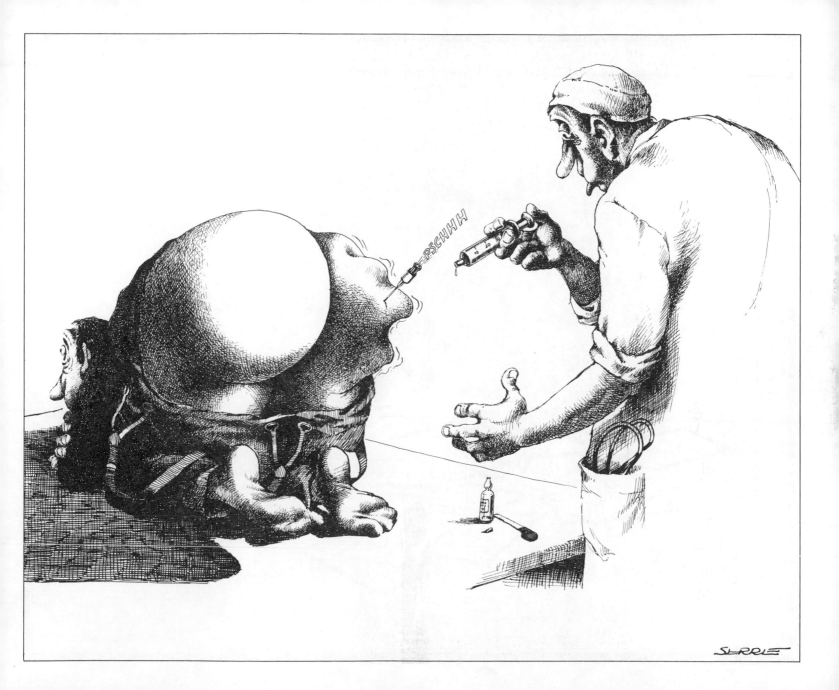